Preface

We spend about 98 percent
else to happen to us. Only .... ourselves inside
what Henri Nouwen called *a fully pregnant moment*, that is,
where we can say to ourselves: "Right now I don't want to be in any
other place, with any other people, or doing anything other than what
I am doing right now!" Mostly we are in one situation, with certain
people, doing certain things, but are waiting for that to end so that
something else or someone else can appear in our lives.

We experience this in many ways: Sometimes we are just waiting
for our bus arrive, for our workday to end, or for a cherished friend to
visit. But at other times our impatience is deeper and we ache for a
new season in our lives, a new person to fall in love with, a more
meaningful career, or for the courage to finally face up to a nagging
problem. We are always waiting.

In that sense, we are always in "advent," a word that comes from
the Latin, *Adventus*, meaning, "coming." We long for someone or
something to come along and bring new meaning into our lives. For
us, as Christians, we see that new meaning in the coming of Christ.

The season of Advent is a time to get in touch with our longing,
our aching, our frustrations. Its crimson color speaks not of penance,
but of desire—and, in desire, we can, as the mystics say, enter into the
loneliness of God and intuit the Kingdom.

RONALD ROLHEISER
TORONTO, CANADA
APRIL 22, 2005

The Rhythm of Love

Saint John of the Cross, in *The Living Flame of Love*, compares our pre-Advent selves to green logs that have been thrown into a fire, the fire of love. Green logs, as we know, do not immediately burst into flame. Rather, being young and full of moisture, they sizzle for a long time before they reach kindling temperature and take into themselves the fire that is around them. So, too, the rhythm of love: only the really mature can burst into flame within community. The rest of us are still too green, too selfish, too damp.

INDEX OPEN

What helps change this is precisely the tension in our lives. In carrying properly our unfulfilled desires, we sizzle and slowly let go of the dampness of selfishness. In carrying tension we come to kindling temperature and are made ready for love.

Pierre Teilhard de Chardin, the Jesuit priest and scientist, noticed that sometimes when you put two chemicals into a test tube they do not automatically unite. They only unite at a higher temperature. They must first be heated to bring about unity. There's an entire anthropology and psychology of love in that image. In order to love we must first be brought to a higher psychic temperature. What brings us there? Sizzling in tension: not resolving the tensions of our lives prematurely; not sleeping with the bride before the wedding.

Advent should not be confused with Lent. The crimson-purple of Advent is not the black-purple of Lent. The former symbolizes yearning and longing, the latter repentance. The spirituality of Advent is about carrying tension without prematurely resolving it so that we do not short-circuit the fullness that comes from respecting love's rhythms. Only when there is enough heat will there be unity. To give birth to what's divine requires the slow patience of gestation.

The sublime has to be waited for. In shorthand, that's Advent.

The spirituality of Advent is about carrying tension without prematurely resolving it.... To give birth to what's divine requires the slow patience of gestation.

The Fire Inside

 In every cell of our bodies and in the very DNA of our souls we ache for someone or something that we have not yet known, ache in a way that leaves us dissatisfied and restless inside our own skins. Our lives always seem too small for us. Moreover—and this is the key—this is God's doing. God is the hand behind this "intolerable shirt of flame," as T. S. Eliot puts it.

The fire inside us comes from the way God made us, namely, to crave the infinite and to be dissatisfied with everything else until that love is consummated. Thus, the fire inside us will never be extinguished simply by attaining the right partner, the right job, the right set of friends, or the right recognition. We will always be on fire.

When Saint Augustine says: "You have made us for yourself, Lord, and our hearts are restless until they rest in you," he is, of course, pointing out why God made us this way. It is a guarantee that we will never be satisfied with anything less than the infinite and the eternal.

Advent celebrates human longing. It asks us not to deny our longings but to enter them, deepen them, and widen them until we undergo a metamorphosis.

Longing shapes the soul in many ways, particularly by helping create the space within us where God can be born. Longing leads us to the stable and the manger of Bethlehem. It carves out a trough into which God can be born.

The fire inside us comes from the way God made us, namely, to crave the infinite and to be dissatisfied with everything else.

Healthy Chastity

In his controversial book, *The Closing of the American Mind*, American educator Allan Bloom suggests that lack of chastity is the leading cause of unhappiness among young people. His thesis runs something like this: "I look at the students I teach, young 20-year-olds, and I see most everything, except happiness. Young people have been everywhere and experienced everything. But they have never had anything sublime in their lives because sublimity depends upon waiting and waiting depends upon chastity. Whatever else they may have had in life, they have never had these: sublimity, waiting, and chastity."

It's interesting to see chastity so defended by a purely secular analyst because today in Western culture chastity is for the most part denigrated in the arts, intellectual circles, and popular culture. Among many of the novelists, critics, and even religious people that I read, preaching chastity isn't just backwards and naive—it's evil, a kind of reverse pornography.

But a healthy chastity is not so much about sex as it is about reverence and respect. It is not just about what we experience, but also about when we experience it. An experience can be wrong simply because it is premature. Chastity, in the end, is about waiting, about trying to carry all things, not just sex, at a more sublime level. To surround anything with proper reverence is to say that it's important.

Waiting and chastity, these are not the virtues of our time. Advent is the season that celebrates these virtues, both by pointing desire towards its adequate object and by teaching us to wait.

An experience can be wrong simply because it is premature.

Loneliness and Longing

 At the end of her Pulitzer Prize-winning novel *Beloved,* Toni Morrison writes: "There is a loneliness that can be rocked....Then there is a loneliness that roams. No rocking can hold it down. It is alive, on its own. A dry and spreading thing that makes the sound of one's own feet going seem to come from a far-off place."

All of us experience this loneliness that roams, that can make us strange to ourselves, that haunts the soul. This kind of loneliness cannot be soothed by a rocking chair. No. It drives us outward, to far-off places.

What's to be gleaned from our wandering? Has loneliness a design? Is there a secret to be learned from our longing?

What we learn is that we are more: more than any moment in our lives, more than any humiliation, more than any achievement, more than the limits of our bodies, marriages, and jobs. Longing takes us beyond. It teaches us—better yet, it lets us touch through desire—God's deep design for each of us. In the end, our longings are about consummation, completeness, harmony, and justice. In our longing, the mystics tell us, we intuit the Kingdom of God.

Advent is about getting in touch with our longing, about letting it teach us that we are more than the limits of our present. It is about coming to a new hope through it, and about getting pregnant through its seed. In longing are the deep seeds of hope.

There is a loneliness that can be rocked. There is also another kind that roams—and this kind drives us into Advent.

---

*In our longing, the mystics tell us,
we intuit the Kingdom of God.*

The Algebra of Advent

 Some years ago, Robert Waller published a book that became a runaway bestseller and an immensely popular movie. Entitled *The Bridges of Madison County*, it fired the romantic imagination in a way that few other stories have in recent times.

The story runs this way:

A photographer for National Geographic magazine is sent out to photograph a series of old bridges in Madison County. Lost, he stops at a farmhouse to ask for directions. As chance would have it, the man of the house has just left for a cattle show. His wife is home alone and she and the photographer instantly sense a deep connection and quickly fall in love. Karma, soul mates, mysticism, whatever, they experience a rare and a powerful affinity. Within hours they are in bed with each other, triggering a love affair that leaves both of them sacramentally scarred for the rest of their lives.

What we are asked to believe is that something truly sublime has taken place, a noble thing worth more than life itself. But can this be so? Can anyone paint a masterpiece or compose a great symphony in a couple of hours? Can sex with someone you met just two hours before be sublime?

Advent is about proper waiting. For something to be sublime there must first be sublimation. Fasting is the necessary prelude to genuine feasting. Greatness of soul is contingent on first nobly carrying tension and not resolving these tensions prematurely. That's the algebra of Advent.

Can anyone paint a masterpiece or
compose a great symphony in a couple of hours?

The Power of a Candle

 In South Africa, prior to the abolition of apartheid, people used to light candles and place them in their windows as a sign of hope, a sign that one day this injustice would be overcome. At one point, the authorities began to crack down on this. It became illegal to have a lit candle in your window, as illegal as carrying a firearm. The irony of this was not missed by the children. They soon had a joke among themselves: "The government is afraid of candles!"

Eventually, as we know, apartheid was overcome. Reflecting upon the forces that helped overthrow it, it is fairly evident that candles, lit religious candles, were more powerful, ultimately, than were firearms. Hope is more powerful than any army.

But what is hope? Many of us mistake wishing for hope. They are not at all the same. Wishing is fantasy, pure and simple. Thus, for example, I can wish that I might win a million dollars, but that is not connected to any reality. It is simple daydreaming. You do not light a candle for a daydream.

Hope is based upon a promise, the promise of God, a promise that says that—human sin and power notwithstanding—justice, peace, love, harmony, gentleness, and graciousness will, eventually, become reality. To light a candle, then, is to say that gentleness and graciousness are ultimately more powerful than threats, torture, and guns. To light a candle is to proclaim to the world that our real allegiance is given to something and to someone beyond them.

In retrospect, the government's paranoia about candles was well-founded. A lit candle is a powerful statement of hope.

Hope is more powerful than any army.

Waiting in Joyful Hope

Pierre Teilhard de Chardin was a man of hope. Indeed his whole vision of things is generally criticized for being too hopeful. So, in trying to explain hope and Advent, allow me a Teilhard story:

Teilhard was a scientist, but he was also a priest and a man whose ultimate vision of things was formed by the gospels. Central to his system of thought was his rock-bottom belief that ultimately all of history, cosmic and human, would come together in Christ into one community of life and love. Yet he was surrounded by colleagues, both Christian and secular, who had a far less hopeful view of things. One day he was challenged this way: "You have an enchanted view of history, believing that everything will one day culminate in a wonderful 'kingdom' of peace and love, but suppose we blow up the world in a nuclear war? What happens to your schema of things then?"

His response to that question is a textbook definition of hope: "If we blow up the world it will be a great tragedy because it will set things back millions of years. But history will still culminate one day in a kingdom of peace and love—not because my theory says so, but because God promised it. In the resurrection God has shown the power to bring this about, despite the things we do."

That's hope, to be able to say, "It might take a million years or longer, but it will happen because God promised it." We, like Teilhard, should be prepared to live in great patience as we wait for God to fulfill his promise.

Ultimately, all of history, cosmic and human,
will come together in Christ.

Groans Too Deep for Words

There is an incredible power, a blind pressure to grow, in all living things.

A friend of mine shares how, after buying a house, he decided to get rid of a bamboo plant in his driveway. He took an axe, cut down the plant, and chopped deep into the earth destroying as much of the roots as he could. Then he poured bluestone, a plant poison, on what remained. Finally, he filled the hole where the plant had been with several feet of gravel which he tamped tightly and paved over with cement.

Two years later, the cement heaved as that bamboo plant began to slowly make its way through the pavement. Its life principle, the blind pressure to grow, was not so easily thwarted by axes, poison, and cement.

Life pushes outward, reaches, and yearns. We see it in adult restlessness, in our greed for experience, in our hunger for sex, in our insatiability, and even in our escapes into daydreams, alcohol, and drugs. We are ever the bamboo plant, blindly pushing upward; the baby, unconsciously crying for milk.

And what is it all for? Why do bamboo plants push blindly through pavements? Why do the hormones of our body and the rages of our soul give us so little peace?

In the end, longing and yearning are the Spirit of God groaning and praying through us. This is what Scripture is talking about when it tells us that when we do not know how to pray, the spirit of God prays through us with groans too deep for words (Romans 8:26). At its root, all longing is for the fruits of the spirit. All life, all eros, and all energy—blind or conscious—yearns for charity, joy, peace, patience, goodness, fidelity, mildness, and the union that chastity can bring.

Whether it's a bamboo plant pushing through a driveway, or a baby crying for milk, or an adult man or woman kneeling in supplication, the yearning is for this. What touches you is what you touch. Advent is the season to touch these longings and to let them touch us.

What touches you is what you touch.

Soul-Building Strength

The word "sublime" comes from the word "sublimation." That's no mere accident of language. The sublime depends upon sublimation: to have great satisfaction, there must first be a great effort; to achieve a great peace, there must first have been a great struggle; and to have a great love, there must first have been a great chastity.

This is true not just for sexuality, but in every area of life. The more soul-wrenching the sublimation, the more soul-exploding the ecstasy. The great novels in every language are powerful precisely because they build upon great tension. It is not in passing that Scripture tells us: "Those who sow in tears will reap in joy!" and that the great mystics tell us that the joys of heaven come after a certain "dark night of the soul."

Our age, for all its unique strengths, tends to have this weakness: it doesn't understand the soul-building power of chastity. We have forgotten the importance of waiting, of longing, of living the sublime fire of tension.

Carlo Carretto, one of the great spiritual writers of our time, spent a number of years living as a hermit, praying in the Sahara desert. When someone asked him what he thought he heard God saying to him in all that silence and after all that prayer, Carretto replied:

"God is telling us: 'Learn to wait-wait-wait for your God! Wait for love, be patient with everything. Everything that is worthwhile must be waited for!'"

Those who sow in tears will reap in joy!

Beware the Noonday Devil

When the desert fathers first formulated a list of what they considered "deadly" sins, they included the sin of sadness. It wasn't until the seventeenth century that it was dropped from the list, replaced by sloth.

How can sadness be a sin? Isn't it a feeling over which we have no control?

The desert fathers spoke of something called *acedia*, "the noonday devil," namely, a sadness that can take you over for no apparent reason. They distinguished this from the sadness that we feel when we have every reason to be sad because we're experiencing a significant loss or breakdown of something. The noonday devil—unlike the devil who strikes at a time of darkness or crisis—hits in broad daylight, when there's seemingly no reason to be sad.

Anything can trigger its entry: an old song on the radio, a beautiful face in a crowd, a reunion party, a half-forgotten lullaby, somebody else's good fortune, a good-bye hug, sorting through old photographs, or even a family occasion that should ideally bring us joy. But how can this be sin?

Sadness itself isn't the sin, but it can be the devil that tempts us toward sin. We can unhealthily luxuriate in sadness so as to rationalize making any further efforts to build up anything. Perhaps that's why the Church eventually called this sin "sloth."

After giving the noonday devil his due, the child of the kingdom turns up her music again, picks up her duties, her hopes, and her prayers, and continues, in joy, to build up the kingdom.

---

*The noonday devil hits in broad daylight,
when there's seemingly no reason to be sad.*

The Unsurrendered Life

 The task of life is ultimately to surrender, as the gospels define this. If you were to take all of Jesus' teachings, all that's said about belief, morality, and piety in the gospels, and boil it down to a single precept, you could put it into one word: surrender.

But to surrender what exactly? The gospels ask us to surrender our individualism, our fears, our security, and our need to stand out and be special. They ask us to surrender our agendas, ambition, anger, and all those things that keep us standing alone or apart.

Sadly, this surrender isn't seen in many lives, even in religious life, especially as we age and we begin to claim more and more private space for ourselves. We need to ask ourselves: Are we becoming too comfortable being alone? Is it healthy to want your own bed for yourself at night, your own space for yourself during the day, and personal fulfillment in your projects and agendas? Is it healthy to want so unshared a life?

It's a biblical tragedy when those of us in mid-life and beyond are so comfortable being alone that sharing our lives with others becomes an addendum to a carefully guarded private world.

Socrates warned that the unexamined life is not worth living. The gospel warns that the unsurrendered life is not biblical.

Are we becoming too comfortable being alone?

The Quest for Sincerity

We all long to be sincere. But sincerity is highly elusive. I was reminded of this recently while having a conversation with a friend of mine who just became a father. "Now that I have a child," he told me, "I want to grow up. I am sick of being bounced around by every fad and politically correct thing to think or say or do. I want to know what I really believe and stand for, but it's difficult. How do I know what is most true within me?" He was struggling to contact his own soul, and he was finding more false layers and pretense there than he had ever imagined.

What does it mean to be sincere? Some dictionaries suggest that sincere comes from two Latin words: *sine* (without) and *caries* (decay). Hence, to be sincere means to be "without corruption." Others suggest that its root is: *sine* (without) and *cero* (to smear, to coat with wax). In this view, to be sincere means to be uncovered, to have a certain nakedness of soul. Both interpretations are true and shed light on its meaning.

To be sincere is to be uncorrupted in mind and heart and soul. It also means to be uncoated, truly yourself, not smeared by pretense, political correctness, or posturing. To be sincere is to be without false props, without a mask, without anything that is not really true to you.

My friend was right to identify the quest for sincerity with the struggle to "finally grow up." Sincerity is about maturity—about truly facing ourselves, each other, and our God.

To be sincere is to be uncoated, truly yourself,
not smeared by pretense or posturing.

Passion and Purity

 Someone once said that the Church does not under-
stand passion while the world does not understand
purity. That might be a rather simplistic generalization
but, to my mind, it contains an important truth. Too
often the Church's concern for purity blocks it from
properly appropriating passion, just as the world's unbridled romance
with passion blinds it to the importance of purity.

Some of the Church's cautiousness with passion is legitimate.
Passion without proper checks has led to an early grave for more than a
few loves and lives. Still, in the end, the Church is too fearful of passion.

On the other hand, the world does not understand purity. Purity
and chastity are regarded with a disapproval bordering on disdain.
Purity is seen as naiveté, lack of nerve, or lack of drive for life.

Living and loving are messy businesses. To be excessively given
over to purity is to be a prude. Our world, in fact, does the Church
a huge favor when it points this out. But the world does itself
immeasurable harm by not understanding the place of purity and
chastity. More emotional chaos, heartbreak, and raging restlessness
result from this lack of understanding than our world admits.

The Church must let go of some of its fears and inhibitions.
It must celebrate the goodness of sexuality and challenge people to
passion, including sexual passion. Conversely, the world must relearn
purity. It must admit how much emotional pain results from
trivializing sex and from denigrating chastity and sexual caution.

Purity and passion make sense only when they are linked and take
their deeper meaning from each other.

Passion without proper checks has led to an early grave
for more than a few loves and lives.

The Celebration of all Celebrations

Many of us, I am sure, are concerned that Christmas has become too much of a secular and commercial event. What used to be a season of waiting to celebrate—Advent—is now a marathon of Christmas parties and shopping. Where is Christ in all of this? How do we put Christ back into Christmas?

Everyone agrees that some of these excesses must be toned down if we are to highlight that this is, after all, Jesus' birthday. For some, the way to put Christ back into Christmas is to eliminate most of what has culturally built up around it—the Christmas tree, Santa Claus, the colored lights, the cards, the carols, the gifts, the endless parties, and the extravagant meals. Christ gets lost in all of this, they contend.

Personally, I don't agree. Christmas, beyond the fact that it is Jesus' birthday and thus fitting cause for the celebration of all celebrations, is the feast of the incarnation, the time to celebrate flesh and the goodness of physical creation! If all the hoopla and color were not there, ironic as this may seem, the meaning of Christmas would not come through to the world, nor to us, as strongly. As John Shea puts it: "A Christmas Spirit that walks around naked will never be noticed. It needs a sprig of holly for allure."

In the end, the spirit of Christmas is helped by all the hoopla surrounding it. The lights, the carols, the colored trees, the gifts, and all that food and drink help highlight the essential truth that God enters into our physical world and makes everything here holy and good.

Christmas is the time to celebrate flesh
and the goodness of physical creation!

Weeping With a Walleye

S ome years ago an American research center conducted an experiment with a walleyed pike. They placed this fish in an aquarium and fed it regularly. Then, after a time, they inserted an invisible glass plate into the aquarium, sealing off part of it. They began to put the walleye's food on the other side of that plate. Every time the fish tried to take some food, it would bump against the glass plate and come away empty.

For quite a while the fish kept swimming up, attempting to take food. Each time, it bumped its mouth and came away empty. Eventually, the walleyed pike stopped trying. It would swim toward the food but, just before striking the glass plate, it would turn and swim slowly away. At this point, the researchers removed the glass plate. But the damage had been done. The fish never ate again. No amount of hunger could drive it to attempt again to eat. It would swim up to the food and, at the last second, turn away, not knowing

that the glass plate was now gone and that it could eat freely. The walleye eventually died of malnutrition, surrounded by food.

This is not meant as a sentimental anecdote designed to make us feel sorry for a poor fish that had the misfortune of falling victim to the cruelties of human experiment. Hearing it does give the heart a sad wrench, but the sorrow it triggers goes much deeper.

All of us know exactly what happened to this walleyed pike and why it eventually stopped eating—and many of us are in danger of dying from a similar malnutrition. We are dying from lack of love in a world where most everyone wants to love, and we are unable to pour out love upon people who are starving for it. There are no glass plates between ourselves and others, and yet we cannot or do not reach out to each other. Something is deeply wrong and we are, all of us, deeply sad.

The value of this story is that it speaks to the soul gently, directly, deeply. It is something not so much to be explained as to be felt. The parable of the walleyed pike helps us name our sorrow.

We are dying from lack of love
in a world where most everyone is starving for it.

Becoming Mild

Saint John of the Cross defined solitude as "bringing the mild into harmony with the mild." That was his way of saying that we will begin to remember the primordial touch of God when, through solitude, we empty our hearts of all that is not mild: namely, noise, anger, bitterness, and jealousy.

Inside each of us there is a church, an oratory, a place of worship, a sanctuary not made by human hands. And it is a gentle place, a virgin place, a holy place, a place where there is no anger, no sense of being cheated, and no need to be competitive.

It is a soft place that can be violated through assault, through a giving of oneself that does not respect oneself—and especially through lying, rationalizing, and the warping and hardening of heart that follows upon that. Conversely, though, it is also a place that can remain inviolate, sacred, and untouched, even through external assault. It is in that place, entered into through solitude and gentleness of spirit, that we have a privileged access to God because that is the place where God has already touched us and where we, however dimly, remember that.

We have been touched by loving hands. The memory of that touch is a brand—warm, dark, gentle. To enter that memory is to lean on the breast of Jesus, just as the beloved apostle did at the Last Supper. From that place, with our ear on the heart of Jesus, we have the truest perspective on our world.

Inside each of us there is a sanctuary
not made by human hands…a gentle, virgin place.

A Humbled Heart

In his book, *The Return of the Prodigal Son*, Henri Nouwen suggests that one of the main things that has to happen in order for us to come to conversion and purity of heart is that we must move from being judge to being repentant sinner.

Our problem is that our own self-righteousness is often hidden from us. In our own eyes we are never the hypocrite or the ones sitting in judgment on somebody else's life. No. We are the honest ones, the compassionate ones, the humble ones. Yet, that is rarely the way we are seen by others, especially by those closest to us. They see in us a moral smugness that offends them.

Thus, for example, if our temperament puts us at home in liberal circles, there is a good chance that we nurse a fair amount of anger against our more conservative and traditional brothers and sisters. We are unaware that they feel judged and rejected by us. The converse is just as true: If we find our home among those of a more conservative mindset, there is a very good chance that we harbor a lot of anger against our more liberal sisters and brothers. Again, we may be unaware that they sense our disdain and disapproval.

Strange how each of us so clearly sees the judgmental attitude in the other and yet is so unaware of how brutally judgmental we ourselves are. Conversion begins when we stop standing as judge in order to kneel as sinner. When we are humble and contrite of heart we will not be spurned by God, nor by each other.

Conversion begins when we stop standing as judge in order to kneel as sinner.

Life's Interruptions

In a biography of C. S. Lewis, A. N. Wilson describes how Lewis' life was, during virtually all of his productive years, interrupted by the demands of his adoptive mother who made him do all the shopping and housework. Lewis' brother Warnie, who also lived in the household (and who generally refused to let his own agenda be so interrupted), laments this fact in his diaries and suggests that Lewis could have been much more prolific had he not been forced to spend countless hours doing domestic chores.

Lewis himself, however, gives a different assessment. Far from being resentful about these interruptions, he's grateful and suggests that it was precisely these domestic demands that kept him in touch with life in a way that other Oxford dons were not. Wilson agrees. He suggests that it was precisely because of these interruptions, which kept Lewis' feet squarely on the ground, that Lewis was able to have such empathic insights into the everyday human condition.

We, too, must look for the hand of God in our interruptions. These often appear as a conspiracy of accidents, but through them God guides and tutors us. If we were totally in control of our own agendas, if we could simply plan and execute our lives according to our own dreams with no unwanted demands, I fear that many of us would slowly and subtly become selfish.

C. S. Lewis once said that we'll spend most of eternity thanking God for those prayers he didn't answer. I suspect we'll also spend a good part of eternity thanking God for those interruptions that derailed our plans.

We must look for the hand of God in our interruptions.
Through them, God guides and tutors us.

Achieving Perfection

 There are two classical concepts of perfection, one Greek and the other Hebrew. In the Greek ideal, to be perfect is to have no deficiencies, no faults, no flaws; it means to be completely whole, true, good, and beautiful. To be perfect, then, is never to sin.

The Hebrew ideal of perfection is quite different. In this mindset, to be perfect simply means to walk with God, despite our flaws. Perfection here means being in the divine presence, in spite of the fact that we are not perfectly whole, good, true, and beautiful.

Our concept of holiness in the West has been shaped by the Greek ideal of perfection. Hence, holiness has been understood as a question of measuring up to a certain benchmark. Such a view is not without its merits. It is a perpetual challenge against mediocrity and laziness: we are always invited to something higher. But such a concept of perfection also has a nasty underside. When perfection means measuring up, we find it hard to forgive ourselves and others for not being God. We carry around a lot of discouragement, guilt and lack of forgiveness because of this.

What God asks is that we bring our helplessness, weakness, and imperfection to him. Like a good parent, he understands that we will make mistakes and disappoint him and ourselves. What he asks is simply that we share our lives with him and that we let him help us when we are powerless to help ourselves.

When perfection means measuring up,
we find it hard to forgive ourselves and others.

God's Presence in Our World

 Daniel Berrigan was once asked to give a conference at a university gathering on "God's Presence in Today's World." I suspect that his talk surprised a number of people in his audience both in brevity and content. He simply told the audience how he spends some time each week sitting by the bed of a boy who is totally incapacitated, physically and mentally.

The young boy cannot speak or express himself to those who come into his room. He lies mute and helpless, by all appearances cut off from any possible communication. Berrigan described how he regularly sits by this young boy's bed to try to hear what he is saying in his silence and helplessness. He explained that the way this young man lies in our world, silent and helpless, is the way God lies in our world. To hear what God is saying we must learn to hear what this young boy is saying.

This is an extremely useful image in helping us understand how the power of God manifests itself in our world. God's power is in the world like that young boy. It does not overpower with muscle, or attractiveness, or brilliance, or grace, as does the speed and muscle of an Olympic athlete or the physical beauty of a young film star.

These latter things—swiftness, beauty, and grace—do reflect God's glory, but they are not the primary way God shows power in this world. God's power in the world is more muted, more helpless, more shamed, and more marginalized. It lies at a deeper level, at the ultimate base of things, and it will, in the end, gently have the final say.

The way this young man lies in our world,
silent and helpless, is the way God lies in our world.

Revealing Our Weaknesses

During the last year of her life, Saint Thérèse of Lisieux correspond regularly with a young man named Maurice who was preparing to become a missionary. While he greatly admired Thérèse and eagerly awaited her advice on things, for a long time he was afraid to tell her about his moral failures. Eventually, he mustered up the courage to share his weaknesses after first confessing the fear that she would see him thereafter as "an object of horror." Thérèse's response is most noteworthy: "It must be that you don't know me well at all, if you are afraid that a detailed account of your faults would lessen the tenderness that I feel for your soul."

God should get more press like this. The fear that this young man experienced is the exact one that all of us perennially have in our relationship with God. Simply put, we are afraid that God's good opinion of us might change should all of our darkest secrets be laid bare.

I know many people, especially young people, who because something is wrong in their lives stop going to church. Generally this expresses itself this way: "Given how I'm living, I would be a hypocrite if I went to church! I'm too honest and humble to go to church right now."

That may sound noble and humble, but it betrays a false understanding of God and ultimately does us no favors. We do not know God very well when we fear coming into God's presence replete with all that is within us, weaknesses as well as strengths. Nothing we do can ever lessen God's tenderness towards us.

---

*Nothing we do can
ever lessen God's tenderness towards us.*

God of Small Things

There is a poem by William Stafford called "Ultimate Problems." It runs like this:

> In the Aztec design God crowds
> into the little pea that is rolling
> out of the picture.
> All the rest extends bleaker
> because God has gone away.
>
> In the White Man design, though,
> no pea is there.
> God is everywhere,
> but hard to see.
> The Aztecs frown at this.
>
> *How do you know He is everywhere?*
> *And how did He get out of the pea?*

INDEX OPEN

You could say that if you are walking the roads of life these days and if you are looking for God, or a piece of God, you should be looking down. For if God is going to be found these days it's going to be in small things. It's going to be close to the ground, it may even be below the ground.

Looking for God these days requires the willingness to investigate the small: to descend, to look down.

Christmas, too, invites us to look down, to descend. Why? Because that is what God did in the Incarnation. He emptied himself, taking on the form of slave. He became small. God became a helpless baby.

Usually, when we look for God we look the other way, toward the sky. We investigate the powerful. We try to ascend. But Christmas invites us to investigate our experience of powerlessness. We should be looking close to the ground, investigating the small, and watching for a baby rolling into the picture.

Christmas invites us to look down, to descend, to investigate the small.

Preparing for Christmas

 Jesus was born in a manger, a place where brute animals, oxen and ass, come to eat. That symbolism is not accidental. It shows us what Jesus will later on explicitly tell us, namely, that his life and his body are food for the life of the world. Christ exists to be eaten—and to be eaten, first of all, by the world, not by the churches. If that is true, then all of church life and ministry exist for that same reason: they are food to be eaten by the world. Christ lay in a manger, a trough, as a sign that he is food for the world.

There is both a challenge and a consolation in that. The challenge is that we, as church communities and as individuals, never become self-absorbed. The Church exists for the sake of the world, not the other way around. Jesus showed us this by lying in a bed of straw. The consolation, if we meditate on the image of Jesus lying in a manger, is that we are imitating Jesus when we feel like we are being eaten up by the demands of ministry, family, justice, and the like.

When I was a child, each Advent my mother used to set out a little manger and ask us kids to place a piece of straw in it every time we made some small sacrifice: "To make a bed for the baby Jesus." That's not bad piety: it's good theology!

Christ lay in a manger, a trough,
as a sign that he is food for the world.

The Hour of Our Death

 I think it was Paulo Freire who once said that we should change the Hail Mary and occasionally pray it this way: Instead of praying "now and at the hour of our death," we should say, "and let me not miss the hour of my death."

I was reminded of it some years ago when I read newspaper accounts of seven Trappist monks who were killed in Algeria. One of them, Dom Christian de Cherge, sent a letter to his family shortly before he was executed. I share some of it here with you.

"If it should happen one day—and it could be today—that I become a victim of terrorism, remember that my life was given to God and to this country and that the one master of all life was not a stranger to this brutal departure. I would like [you] to pray for me…and to be able to associate this death with so many other equally violent ones which are allowed to fall into the indifference of anonymity. My life has no more value than any other. Nor any less.

"This is what I shall be able to do, if God wills it: to immerse my gaze in that of the Father and to contemplate with him his children of Islam as he sees them, all shining with the glory of Christ, fruit of his passion, filled with the gift of the Spirit whose secret joy will always be to establish communion and to refashion the likenesses, playing with the differences."

This letter is a testament of faith and forgiveness. Dom Christian de Cherge did not miss the hour of his death.

Let me not miss the hour of my death.

The Breath of God

The ancients believed that there was a soul in everything and that this soul, which was God's breath, held everything together and gave it meaning. They did not understand, as we do today, the workings of the infra-atomic world. They could not explain these things scientifically, but they recognized that some form of love exists inside all things, however inanimate. For them the breath of God was one force. The physical and spiritual worlds were not set against each other.

We need to understand things in that same way. We need to let the Holy Spirit, in all his and her fullness, animate our lives. What this means concretely is that we must not let ourselves be energized and driven too much by one part of the Holy Spirit to the detriment of other parts of that same Spirit.

Thus, our lives should not be about sex in the absence of commitment, pleasure in the absence of conscience, or artistic or professional achievement in the absence of personal fidelity. Especially, they should not be about a good life for ourselves in the absence of justice for everyone.

Conversely, we should be suspicious of ourselves when we have morality without passion or creativity, or when our conscience has a problem with pleasure. One spirit is the author of all of these things. Hence, equal attention must be paid to each.

We should be suspicious of ourselves
when we have morality without passion,
or when our conscience has a problem with pleasure.

Shimmering with Divinity

 God has not promised us a life free from pain, sickness, loneliness, oppression, and death. What God has promised in the incarnation is that he will be with us in that pain. That is something quite different. That is why our Savior's name is Emmanuel, a name which means God-is-with-us.

Cardinal Avery Dulles aptly put it this way: "Jesus enables us to believe that human life, with all its contradictions, is the place where God is preeminently found. Unlike every other mythology, the myth of the Incarnation gives us strength to face up to the harsh realities of our fragmented world, to feel and to transmit the touch of God's reconciling love. The Incarnation does not provide us with a ladder by which to escape from the ambiguities of this life and scale the heights of heaven. Rather it enables us to burrow deep into the heart of the planet earth and find it shimmering with divinity."

As a Christian, I do not ask God to exempt me from the human condition. My life is meaningful precisely when I sense God's presence in the midst of my suffering, sicknesses, loneliness, and pain. My faith allows me to stand inside of every reality in my life, positive and negative, and to see some meaning in it.

In the end, to have faith in God is to have faith that God is with us.

To have faith in God is
to have faith that God is with us.

Heavenly Fantasies

 More than a few people are shocked by sexual imagery when it is applied to heaven. However, it is precisely the image of sexual intercourse that is dominant in the way the great Christian mystics, including John of the Cross and Teresa of Avila, describe heaven. In the end, the vision is one of wholeness, consummation, and of love without limit.

I highlight this here because seldom are we taught that our fantasies and dreams can be the place where we intuit the meaning of salvation. In our daydreams, the normal rules of the world are bypassed and nothing is impossible: We can fly! Our marriages are perfect and our sexual embraces are deep. We accomplish marvelous things irrespective of our athletic, artistic, or practical limitations. We can be that one-in-a-million artist, athlete, movie star, or saint.

Finally, in our healthy fantasies we are always at our best and our noblest. We are never petty, narrow, and small in our daydreams. We are paragons of virtue and nobility—generous, kind, deeply loving, and most gracious.

Thomas Aquinas distinguished between two kinds of union. For him, you could be in union with something either through possession or through desire. In our fantasies—indeed most often in those that are so sensual, so narcissistic, and so private that we are ashamed of them—we are given a privileged opportunity to understand what salvation looks and feels like.

Seldom are we taught that our fantasies and dreams can be the place where we intuit the meaning of salvation.

The Mangers in Our World Today

 As we prepare ourselves to celebrate Christmas, let me speak of one of the aspects of this feast that we too rarely examine. The God who's born into our world at Christmas is always being born into a world that hasn't got room for him. Thomas Merton once put it this way:

"Into this world, this demented inn, in which there is absolutely no room for him at all, Christ has come uninvited. But because he cannot be at home in it, because he is out of place in it and yet must be in it, his place is with those others for whom there is no room. His place is with those who are discredited, who are denied the status of persons."

That's a message our culture needs to hear. The poor more easily make a place for God in their lives. Their stables and mangers are more available for God's birth than are our homes, condos, and hospitals—not to mention our boardrooms, talk shows, college classrooms, and other centers of influence.

In our lives and in our world, perennially, there's no room at the inn, no place to welcome the God who wants to be born there. As it was at the first Christmas, the Christ child today must be born outside our cities, among the poor. Hence, to find him we must let ourselves be led by the poor, the children, or by some other guiding star to the mangers in our world today.

The poor more easily make a place for God in their lives.
We must let ourselves be led by them
to the mangers in our world today.

Born into the Ordinary

After the birth of Christ, we need not look to the extraordinary, the spectacular or the miraculous to find God. God is now found where we live—in our kitchens, at our tables, in our wounds, and in each other's faces.

That is hard to believe and always has been. When Jesus was on earth, virtually no one believed he was the Messiah, precisely because he was so ordinary, so unlike what they imagined God to be. They had expected a superstar, a king, someone who would turn the world rightfully upside down. Preaching meekness and gentleness, Jesus didn't live up to those expectations.

It is curious that Scripture refuses to describe what Jesus looked like. It never tells us whether he was short or tall, with beard or without, had light or dark hair, had blue or brown eyes. Neither does it ever assign to him anything extraordinary in terms of psychological

GENE PLAISTED, OSC

countenance. For example, it never tells us that when Jesus entered a room his eyes were so penetrating and his gaze so awesome that people knew they were in the presence of someone extraordinary. No. In terms of his appearance, Jesus apparently wasn't worth describing. He looked like everyone else. Even after the resurrection, he is mistaken for a gardener, a cook, a traveler.

Things haven't changed much in two thousand years. Seldom does Christ meet expectations. We, like his contemporaries, are constantly looking beyond the ordinary, beyond the gardener, the cook, and the traveling stranger, to try to find a miraculous Christ. It is for this reason that we fly off to Fatima or Lourdes to see a spot where the Blessed Virgin might have cried, but fail to see the significance of the tears shed at our own breakfast table. We are intrigued by a Padre Pio who had the wounds of Christ on his hands, but fail to see the wounds of Christ in those suffering around us or in our own emotional and moral wounds.

We pray for visions, but seldom watch a sunset. We marvel at the gift of tongues, but are bored listening to babies. We look for Christ everywhere, except in the place where the incarnation took place: our flesh.

Love is a thing that happens in ordinary places—in kitchens, at tables, in bedrooms, in workplaces, in families, in the flesh. God abides in us when we abide there. Through the Incarnation, God crawls into ordinary life and invites us to meet him there.

We are intrigued by a Padre Pio who had the wounds of Christ on his hands, but fail to see the wounds of Christ in those suffering around us.

Joy and Pain

 In this life there is no such thing as a clear-cut, pure joy. Everything comes mixed. As Henri Nouwen once put it: Every bit of life is touched by a bit of death. In every satisfaction there is limitation; in every embrace, there is distance; in every success, there is the fear of jealousy; behind every smile, there is a tear.

It is because of this strange paradox that all the events within Christ's life and within our own lives are experienced in such a mixed way. For example, when the Virgin Mary, a young mother, comes before Simeon in the Temple, he looks at her and her child and says: "This child is destined for the fall and rise of many, a sign that will be contradicted…and a sword too will pierce your own heart." An interesting thing to say to a young mother! We have our own experiences of this. Many is the mother who cries at her daughter's wedding, even though it is a joyful occasion. A sword is piercing her heart, too.

Joy and pain both lie at the heart of what it means to be human. In terms of a biblical definition, the human being might well be defined as a being of joy, living in pain. And in the end that is what separates us from the rest of creation. The paradoxical connection between joy and pain points us toward eternity.

What Christ promises us is not a life on this earth without pain, but an eventual joy that no one can ever take from us.

Every bit of life is touched by a bit of death.
Behind every smile, there is a tear.

Un-Ordinary Time

 As human beings we have an irresistible, healthy, and God-given need to make festival, to have un-ordinary time, to have carnival. Christmas is sabbath, sabbatical, in the true biblical sense—and also the only sabbatical most of us will ever get! There are seasons in life, and these should be regular, meant solely for enjoyment, for color, for tinsel. There is even the occasional time for a bit of excess. Jesus voiced that when his followers objected to a woman's excess in anointing him. All cultures, whether poor or rich, have always had times of festival where, spoken or unspoken, they took seriously the words: The poor you will always have with you, but today it is time to celebrate! Christmas is this time.

John Shea, in his marvelous little book on Christmas, tells the story of a family who decided one year to have an alternative Christmas. They did not put up a tree, string any lights, play any carols, or exchange any gifts. They met for a simple, quiet meal on Christmas day. Asked by friends how it went, one member of the family replied, "It was pleasant." Another member, perhaps speaking more honestly, said, "It was an existential abyss."

There is a God-given press within human nature that pushes us to celebrate, and this is a healthy pressure. It keeps us aware that we are not meant for gloom but that we are destined for more, much more, than our poor lives can give us just now. The excess of carnival, of festival, of Christmas, teaches us this lesson.

We are destined for more, much more,
than our poor lives can give us just now.

Christmas Joy

 My fiftieth year has come and gone but at Christmas I'm a child again, delighting in the creche, the lights, the carols, the Christmas tree. I've always loved Christmas, loved everything about it. Partly this is simple luck and has nothing really to do with Christmas as a religious event. I've always been handed the long straw as regards Christmas joy.

As a child, this was the most special time of the year for our family. At Christmas, everyone came home and the family had its major reunion for the year. All the stops were pulled. We got to spend a week eating all the best foods we could afford (and some which we couldn't). A tree and beautiful lights livened up our old house, peaceful carols played non-stop on our Fleetwood phonograph, and we enjoyed unhurried time with each other, doing nothing but enjoying life. What kid, or adult, shouldn't love this? Part of the luck, too, unlike for some of my friends, is that none of my Christmas days, so far, have ever been interrupted by tragedy, the death of a loved one, or by serious illness.

Moreover, our family was religious. Christmas was, first of all, a spiritual time for us. There was special food, but there was also special prayer. Santa never visited our home. Instead the Christ-child brought us our gifts and his visits were just as ingeniously arranged by my parents as Santa's visits are arranged by other parents.

Karl Rahner, fine theologian that he was, used to say: In Christmas, God gives us permission to be happy! Why decline the offer?

At Christmas, I'm a child again,
delighting in the creche, the lights, the carols,
and the Christmas tree.

The Creche

When Pablo Picasso was a young child, a huge fire broke out in the city where his family lived. A night of chaos followed with people rushing about the streets shouting: there was commotion and anarchy everywhere. Later, as an adult, Picasso recalled that night and described how, through all that chaotic night, he sat snug inside a harness-vest on his father's chest, watching all the turmoil from a secure, protected space. He felt no fear, only wonder, as he took it all in. He was snug and safe.

I have a warm memory, too, about being a child and feeling snug and secure in a world full of cold and chaos. My memory has to do with Christmas Eve and going to church and seeing, in the crib at the front of church, the baby, Jesus. Our parish still has the same crib, all these years later, and I still see parents bringing their young children forward to the creche to look at the nativity scene.

To a child's eyes, all the peace promised by Isaiah's vision is there: A little baby, the prince of peace, the God of the whole universe, sleeps peacefully in the straw, surrounded by a loving mother and an attentive father and praying shepherds and animals who are calm and still. To a child, the nativity scene is the snug harness of safety.

When a child sees and feels this, that child walks away from the creche with a mystic's eye and a mystic's heart, secure in the knowledge that the God of the poor, the peaceful, the little, and the innocent rules the world.

To a child's eyes, all the peace promised
by Isaiah's vision is in the creche.

Symbols of Love and Light

 The Christmas symbols are still very meaningful to me. I love the creche, the lights, the carols and the tree. Moreover, as I get older, the meaning of these things, especially the creche and the lights, is becoming more clear, and dear, to me.

The creche is an image of heaven. Everything about it radiates peace, love, fulfillment, the end of longing, the lack of tears. It's an icon of Isaiah's vision of the lion lying down with the lamb, of God wiping away every tear. The baby, appropriately enough, is always asleep because the whole scene depicts eternal rest, namely, what it means to sleep "in heavenly peace." "Silent Night," beautifully sung, combined with a creche is as good a holy picture of heaven as you'll get this side of eternity.

The Christmas lights represent the light and warmth of God. In the Northern Hemisphere, Christmas comes just after the winter solstice, that is, pretty well on the coldest, darkest day of the year. Originally, before electricity, lights were real fire, bringing both heat and light. The idea, then, is that just when it's darkest and coldest, God's light and warmth break into the world. The custom of having midnight mass, which some trace to Saint Francis of Assisi, has the same rationale. At the coldest, darkest hour on the coldest, darkest day of the year, the warmth and light of God break through.

These beautiful symbols help celebrate Jesus' birth and announce that God's light and love have come into the world.

The song "Silent Night" combined with a creche
is as good a holy picture of heaven
as you'll get this side of eternity.

Sharon's Christmas Prayer

Among John Shea's poems, one finds a wonderful
little piece titled "Sharon's Christmas Prayer."
With his permission, I'd like to share it
with you here.

> She was five, sure of the facts,
>   and recited them with slow solemnity,
>   convinced every word was revelation.
>   She said
> they were so poor
> they had only peanut butter and jelly sandwiches to eat
> and they went a long way from home
> without getting lost.
> The lady rode a donkey, the man walked,
> and the baby was inside the lady.
> They had to stay in a stable
> with an ox and an ass (hee-hee)
> but the Three Rich Men found them
> because a star lited the roof.
> Shepherds came and you could
> pet the sheep but not feed them.
> Then the baby was borned.
> And do you know who he was?
>   Her quarter eyes inflated to silver dollars.
> The baby was God.
>   And she jumped in the air,
>   whirled round, dove into the sofa,
>   and buried her head under the cushion,
>   which is the only proper response
>   to the Good News of the Incarnation.

Who Would Have Thought It?

S
ome years ago, I visited the Holy Land. It's a strangely different place, and history leaps out at you from every rock. Ancient things from beyond our time seem to surface there and mix with the things of today. When you stand in its sacred spots, you begin to understand why Moses was told to take off his shoes.

I walked its ground, barefoot in soul, for several weeks. Of all the things I saw, including the tomb of Christ, none touched me as deeply as the Church of the Visitation. It stands in sharp contrast to many of

JACOPO PONTORMO, *THE VISITATION*, SAN MICHELE, CARMIGNANO

the other churches that mark the key events in Christ's life. It is a very modest building and is basically unadorned. However, behind the altar there is a painting that depicts the scene of the Visitation. It was this painting of Elizabeth's visit to Mary that struck me so deeply.

In the scene, two peasant women, both pregnant, greet each other. Everything about it suggests smallness and obscurity. What you see is two rather plain-looking women, standing in the dust of an unknown village. Nothing suggests that either of them, or anything that they are doing or carrying, is out of the ordinary. Yet—and this is the genius of the painting—that littleness makes you automatically ask the question: "Who would have thought it? Who could ever have imagined that these two women, in this obscure town, in this obscure place, in this obscure time, were carrying inside of themselves something that would radically and forever change the world? Who would have guessed that they were gestating the Christ and the Prophet?"

There is a lesson in that. Never underrate, in terms of world importance, anyone who is pregnant with promise. Never underestimate the impact in history of silent, hidden gestation. The painting in the Church of the Visitation tells us that what changes the world is what we give birth to in obscurity and dust, within the frustration of lives that will always seem too small for us. If we allow ourselves to become pregnant with hope and carry that hope through a long, humble gestation process, we will impact the world.

May the lesson of the Incarnation touch us deeply and bless our lives!

What changes the world is what we give birth to in obscurity and dust, within the frustration of lives that will always seem too small for us.

Christ Hidden Beneath the Whitewash

There is a story told in Holland, perhaps more mythical than true. It runs this way:

There was an old church. For many years, upon entering it, everyone would stop and bow in the direction of a whitewashed wall. Nobody knew exactly why anybody did that, but everyone had been doing it for such a long time that nobody questioned it. It was tradition. Besides, there was something fitting about doing it. It felt right.

One day, the parish decided to renovate the church. Among other things, they began to strip the paint and whitewash off the old walls. While doing this, they discovered traces of a painting on the wall that everyone bowed to. They became very careful and peeled off the paint gently so as not to damage what was beneath it. Slowly, a very beautiful, centuries-old painting of Christ emerged. Nobody alive was old enough to have actually seen it before. It had been whitewashed over for at least a century. Yet everyone had been bowing to it, not knowing why, but sensing that there was good reason for the reverence.

There is a Christmas lesson in that. Western culture still bows towards the crib of Bethlehem. We may be post-Christian in our beliefs, our attitudes, our ethics, and our politics, but we still celebrate Christmas. Like the people in that church in Holland, we are not really clear any more as to why we are doing what we are doing. There is not much conscious faith left in our Christmas celebrations, just an habitual response to a tradition.

But—as the story of the painting recovered in a church in Holland can teach us—that's not all bad. It's better than not bowing to the wall at all. At least we still have the sense that there is something special beneath the whitewash.

If we are among the ones who still know that there is a painting of Christ behind the whitewash, our response should not be one of cynicism. The Christian choice at Christmas is not: do we celebrate or not? Of course we celebrate and we should be happy that the world is still making a big deal out of Christ's birth, even if it isn't so clear any more as to why.

Our task is not to stop the bowing or the celebration. Our task is to help peel off the whitewash, to help restore the painting beneath it, and to tell the story of who did the painting and why.

You criticize the bad by the practice of the better. The best way to help our culture to celebrate Christmas properly is not by criticizing how it celebrates, nor by ourselves ceasing to celebrate, but by celebrating in a better way.

Let our joy exceed that of the commercial world! Let our bow be deeper and more aware of the marvelous gift that's behind the whitewash: the gift of the Incarnation of our God!

Our task is not to stop the bowing or the celebration.
Our task is to help peel off the whitewash and
to tell the story of the Incarnation.

DAYBREAKS

Advent is a time to get in touch with our heartfelt longings and deepest desires. It is a time to give new birth to the soul as we wait in hope for the joyous celebration of the reality of Christ's presence among us—here and everywhere, now and for all time.

Daybreaks is a journey through the seasons of Advent and Christmas. Popular spiritual writer Father Ron Rolheiser guides the journey with provocative insights and daily reflections on the mystery of the Incarnation.

All who seek refuge from the commercial distractions of the holiday season will find a welcome spiritual retreat in the pages of *Daybreaks*. These daily reflections open the door to the wonder and beauty of Advent and Christmas, and lead to the true peace and joy that only Christ can give.

Father Ron Rolheiser is a member of the Missionary Oblates of Mary Immaculate and president of the Oblate School of Theology in San Antonio, Texas. He is an internationally recognized community-builder, retreat director, and author. Father Rolheiser's weekly column is carried by more than fifty newspapers worldwide. He is the author of the best-selling books *The Shattered Lantern* and *The Holy Longing*.

© 2005, Liguori Publications, Liguori, MO 63057-9999
Imprimatur: Most Reverend Robert J. Hermann,
Archdiocesan Administrator, Archdiocese of St. Louis
Printed in the USA. All rights reserved.
To order, call 800-325-9521. Visit us on the Web at liguori.org.
"Ultimate Problems" copyright 1987, 1988 by the Estate of William Stafford.
Reprinted from The Way It Is: New & Selected Poems
with the permission of Graywolf Press, Saint Paul, Minnesota.
"Sharon's Christmas Prayer," copyright 1977 by John Shea.
Used with the permission of the author.
Editor: Alicia von Stamwitz

Liguori
ONE LIGUORI DRIVE
LIGUORI MO 63057-9999

Cover design: Wendy Barnes
Cover Image: Index Open

13G
PAULINE BOOKS & MEDIA
£1.25

ISBN 978-0-7648-1337-5

50000>

9 780764 813375